Yosemite evokes a sense of inspiration, wonder, and mystique. Some call it magical. The constant interplay of water, weather, and light on its sublime scenery captures forms, textures, and colors of both breathtaking splendor and serene subtlety. Among the Earth's distinctive places, this showcase occupies a special niche in the human spirit, affording experiences that are as personal and individual as the people touched by its bewitching power.

Beyond the placid Merced
River, its flow ebbing in late
summer, morning mist slowly
releases its grip on Leidig
Meadow as sunlight begins
to bathe Yosemite Valley.

Yosemite National Park, *located in central California, was established in 1890; it preserves Yosemite Valley, giant sequoias, other forests, and High Sierra wilderness.*

Front cover: Yosemite Falls, photo by Gail Bandini. Inside front cover: Sentinel Rock in autumn, photo by Josef Muench. Page 1: Along Illilouette Creek, and Pages 2/3: Early morning on the Merced River, photos by Dianne Dietrich Leis. Pages 4/5: Sawtooth Ridge, photo by Carr Clifton.

Edited by Cheri C. Madison.
Book design by K. C. DenDooven.

Second Printing, 1991
in pictures YOSEMITE The Continuing Story
© 1991 KC PUBLICATIONS, INC.

LC 91-60042. ISBN 0-88714-057-2.

in pictures

Yosemite
The Continuing Story

by Leonard McKenzie

Leonard McKenzie has been Chief of Interpretation at Yosemite National Park since 1974. After working two summers as a National Park Service student trainee before earning a biology degree from the University of New Mexico, Len subsequently served in different interpretive capacities at Yosemite, Lassen Volcanic, Everglades, and Mammoth Cave national parks and Assateague Island National Seashore.

GEORGE J. SCHWARTZ

National park areas are special landscapes set aside by acts of Congress to protect and preserve features of national significance that are generally categorized as scenic, scientific, historical, and recreational. As Americans, we are joint caretakers of these unique places, and we gladly share them with visitors from around the world.

Embracing 1,169 square miles in the central Sierra Nevada, Yosemite National Park displays a dramatic landscape that belies its origins. Over millions of years, as uplifts forced the land skyward, weathering and erosion removed the sedimentary layers of a former sea floor. Streams and rivers, then glaciers, slowly but inexorably sculptured the granites that had formed beneath the sedimentary overburden. The scenic masterwork we call Yosemite—its spectacular landforms and its diverse mix of plants and wildlife—is still changing, constantly subjected to the interplay of natural forces and ecological dynamics.

Yosemite's namesake valley, which John Muir called "one glorious flower garden," is the park's centerpiece. Its vertical scale challenges the imagination.

Yosemite: the Valley—
Water: the Force

Anthropologist Loren Eiseley wrote, "If there is magic on this planet, it is contained in water." The lifeblood of any biological system as well as a powerful cutting force, water transforms landscapes and sustains all life on and in them. Perhaps it is water, more than any other feature, that endows Yosemite, especially its wondrous valley, with its mystical allure. From thundering waterfalls, several of them among the world's highest, to sparkling lakes, from rollicking torrents to quiescent pools, water emphatically punctuates Yosemite's predominantly granite land base. Indeed, water in its liquid and solid forms is the primary agent that fashioned and still shapes Yosemite's scenery. As crustal plate movements and intense pressures within the Earth intermittently uplifted the Sierra Nevada along a fault zone on the mountain range's eastern edge, its tilt toward the west progressively steepened. Rivulets flowing into streams that converged into rivers gradually knifed into the rock to engrave a dendroid pattern of drainage channels into a rolling landscape. Then, as the range continued to rise and the gradient increased, master streams such as the Merced River deepened their canyons more rapidly, slicing pathways for Ice Age glaciers.

Although Yosemite Valley's alluvial floor is relatively ▲ *flat, sloping sections quicken the flow of the Wild and Scenic Merced River that meanders through it. Spawned partially on 13,114-foot Mt. Lyell, Yosemite's highest peak, "The River of Our Lady of Mercy" (translated from the original Spanish name) drains a large watershed. It tumble's from the Sierra crest through steep-sided canyons and past the valley's exalted landmarks to dammed Lake McClure west of the park.*

▲ *Runoff from snowmelt in the Sierra climaxes in April and May, swelling streams to torrential proportions and waterfalls to roaring cataracts. The fresh spring foliage of white alder, black cottonwood, bigleaf maple, and western azalea brightens the banks of the Merced River. Riparian (streamside) plants play a critical role in stabilizing riverbank soils against the onslaught of rushing water; where human foot traffic denudes banks, soil erosion may become excessive.*

Glaciers—
Ice on the Move

ED COOPER

▲ **Commencing about**
2 million years ago, when the climate turned colder, moving ice fields called glaciers crept downslope from the Sierra crest in at least three, probably more, episodes. Quarrying and scraping the land, fingers of debris-laden ice advanced across the rock and, like sandpaper, abraded it, leaving glacial polish and striations as evidence of their tracks when they retreated.

▲ **At Olmsted Point, named for Frederick Law Olmsted,**
designer of New York City's Central Park as well as first chairman of the Yosemite Park Commission (1864-1866), randomly strewn boulders seemingly sprinkled over the scoured bedrock offer convincing testimony for the power of moving ice. Captured and transported from source points between here and the Sierra crest, these glacial erratics were deposited when the last ice sheet melted. Half Dome looks oddly different from this Tioga Road vista.

TOM ALGIRE

RUSS FINLEY

▲ **O**verridden by at least one and perhaps several thick glaciers, Liberty Cap (right) and Mt. Broderick (center) exhibit the asymmetric shape of *roches moutonnées. Ice lumbered smoothly over the solid upstream incline of each knob and plucked away granite blocks on the jointed (fractured) lee side, steepening and roughening its surface. The "back" side of Half Dome overshadows both peaks.*

Although glaciers ▷ *assaulted Royal Arches and North Dome on the north wall of Yosemite Valley, it is chiefly exfoliation that accounts for their curvature. Sheet joints essentially parallel to the surface topography create layered shells that slowly weather, disintegrate, and spall off, thus rounding angular landforms.*

Half Dome

Recognized ▷
universally as
Yosemite's hallmark,
Half Dome stands 4,800
feet above the eastern
end of Yosemite Valley.
The Ahwahneechee, the
Indian people who lived
in the valley, called it
Tis-sa-ack, a woman
turned to stone because
of her anger; her tears of
sadness are still visible
on her light-colored face
on the sheet wall. Half
Dome never really had
another "half." In fact,
most of the formation is
still intact. Although
glacial ice did not reach
the upper 900 feet of the
dome, glaciers
undermined its vertically
jointed northwest side
and frost-wedging pried
off the overhead rock.

ED COOPER

DIANNE DIETRICH LEIS

Cables allow ◢
hikers to climb the
60-degree northeast
slope to the summit of
Half Dome, here partially
obscured by
Quarter Dome.

FRED HIRSCHMANN

◀ **S**unset suffuses
"Tis-sa-ack" in
alpenglow,
accentuating its
textures and patterns.
The 2,000-foot face
hosts both rock
climbers and nesting
peregrine falcons.

Yosemite Falls— In the Four Seasons

▽ **The camera lens and** photographic angle distort the relative heights of Upper and Lower Yosemite Falls from the short trail to their base. Separated from the Upper Fall by the Middle Cascades (675 feet), the Lower Fall (320 feet) is less than one-fourth its senior partner's height—yet twice Niagara Falls's.

RUSS FINLEY

△ **Yosemite Falls, the world's fifth highest** waterfall at 2,425 feet in total height, hits its percussive crescendo when stream runoff peaks in late spring, the beneficiary of melting snow. The Upper Fall plunges 1,430 feet in a single drop. Draining a watershed of largely bare, nonabsorbent granite, Yosemite Creek joins the Merced River in Yosemite Valley. Rock that spalled off the cliff above the cleft to the left of the Upper Fall in 1980 covered about a mile of the falls trail.

RAYE SANTOS

By late summer, when little snow remains in the high country, Yosemite Falls has dwindled to a trickle—or dried up completely. Countless episodes of frost-wedging gradually loosened layers of granite that fell away from the cliff to the left of the Upper Fall in 1975; additional rockfall enlarged the light gray patch the following year.

RUSS FINLEY

Occasional snowfall adds a ▷ dimension of fantasy and quietude to the valley and its features. Snow and frozen mist cling to the cliff before melting or breaking off as the day warms. Much heavier snowfall higher in the watershed will feed Yosemite Falls the following spring and summer.

El Capitan—Truly a Rock of the Ages

ED COOPER

▲ *El* Capitan—"the chief"—symbolizes strength and durability. Posing imperially at Yosemite
*Valley's west gates, its summit about 3,600 feet above the valley floor, the massive, solid "El Cap" resisted the
grinding, gouging force of glaciers. Endangered peregrine falcons reappeared in Yosemite in 1978 after an
absence of many years, their population threatened by pesticides. They now nest on the North American
wall (the east face), recognizable by the darker, fine-grained diorite shaped roughly like this continent. A
program of "nest augmentation" is aiding their recovery. The large overhang near "Central America" shelters
an 80-foot ponderosa pine. Rock climbers ascend this monumental cliff via many routes.* ▶

Waterfalls—Yosemite's Signature

▼ **Waterfalls are Yosemite's signature. Plummeting from hanging valleys high above** trunk canyons such as Yosemite Valley or bouncing down precipitous slopes over boulders and ledges, they put the exclamation point on this landscape where nature makes an eloquent declaration of beauty and power. Perhaps nowhere is the raw power of a tempestuous river more forcefully displayed than at the brink of Nevada Fall, where the Merced River funnels through a narrow chute to plunge 594 feet in a snowy, frothy plume over the upper step of the Giant Stairway. Like its downstream neighbor, Vernal Fall, Nevada runs year-round, fed by snowfields and glaciers in the upper Merced River basin. A misstep on wet rock or entering the current upstream of the fall has an almost inevitably fatal outcome.

▲ **A transitory stream on the** eastern buttress of El Capitan, Horsetail Fall flows in late winter and early spring. Not uncommonly, swirling wind on the cliff face joins forces with late-afternoon sunlight to enhance its filmy, ethereal quality.

◀ **The lower step in the Giant** Stairway—cliffs quarried by glaciers that scooped out vertically jointed rock when they descended the Merced River canyon—Vernal Fall, 317 feet high and 80 feet wide at peak flow, attracts thousands of hikers each summer day.

Fire—A Force of Nature

◀ **Fire has been** integral to Sierra Nevada ecosystems for thousands of years. Sparked by lightning, intermittent fires cleansed forests, thinning out understory plants and reducing fuels, opening the canopy to sunlight, fostering diverse regrowth and enhancing conditions for wildlife, cultivating a seedbed, recycling nutrients into the soil, and inhibiting forest pathogens. Most were slow-burning ground fires; occasionally, under extreme conditions, hot fires scorched the land. In the early 1970s, after years of total fire suppression, the National Park Service acknowledged the ecological role of fire, establishing prescribed burning (deliberately set management fires) and prescribed natural fire programs.

◀ *At Yosemite's higher elevations, where cooler, moister conditions normally prevail and vegetation is sparser, natural fires are generally monitored and allowed to run their course. Fires that threaten to burn out of control are contained or suppressed, as are all human-caused fires and low-elevation natural fires. Discretion and professional judgment are crucial in fire management.*

▽ **On August 7, 1990, lightning strikes on steep,** *low-elevation slopes just inside the park's western boundary ignited fires in dense, dry growth. Firefighters were dispatched immediately, but strong winds spread the blazes quickly, outpacing the crews' ability to hold them in check. The fires burned about 26,000 acres, leaving a mosaic of totally and partially burned, as well as untouched, vegetation.*

△ **Within several weeks of the** *1990 fires, new life was sprouting, even in intensely burned areas. Rebirth and renewal were under way. Over the next 10 to 20 years natural regeneration will flourish, transforming apparent devastation to luxuriant gardens of rich biological diversity. Fire is not so much a force of destruction as it is an agent of change, the one constant in nature.*

The Moods of the Valley

ED COOPER

▲ **Standing apart from the** south wall of the valley, the product of exfoliation and frost-splitting of vertically jointed granite, one of two Cathedral Spires pierces a typically deep-blue Sierran sky. The resemblance to a church steeple is obvious!

▲ **Morning light and an unruffled Merced River accent the** Three Brothers, which symbolize the sons of Tenaya, the last chief of the Ahwahneechee. Eagle Peak, its apex never glaciated, represents the eldest son. Parallel master joints, or fracture planes, account for the uniform angle of the westward-tilting slopes. Like a rampart, this otherwise-solid mass defied the plowing, gouging incursions of glaciers in their Ice Age encounters.

DENNIS FLAHERTY

◀ **Day's early light unveils a** crystalline cloak of frost on corn lilies and grasses in high, moist meadows beyond the valley's rims. The corn lilies' curled leaves, still wrapped around unseen stems that may grow to six feet in height, indicate late spring or early summer. Yet, even then, a near-freezing nighttime chill is not uncommon at higher elevations.

GARY LADD

▲ **Ground fog breaks its gentle hold on the valley floor, dissolving** into gauzy gossamers on a spring morning. This quiet interlude heralds a busy day in Yosemite; off-season visitation has mushroomed in recent years. A project to restore the Merced River's ecosystem, including its trampled banks, is under way.

Overleaf: Tenaya Lake ▶ glistens in its glacially gouged basin. Photo by Jeff Gnass.

The High Sierra Country

If the valley is the heart of Yosemite, the high country is its soul. "Thousands of tired, nerve-shaken, over-civilized people are beginning to find out that going to the mountains is going home; that wildness is a necessity; and that mountain parks and reservations are useful not only as fountains of timber and irrigating rivers, but as fountains of life."

Written in 1898, John Muir's words are no less fitting today. Reaching summits more than 13,000 feet in elevation on the Sierra crest, most of it formally designated as wilderness in 1984, the high country of Muir's "Range of Light" beckons hikers and backpackers to sample his "measureless mountain days" on 800 miles of park trails.

***Spring arrives late** ▽ in the high country. After a "normal" winter, snow lingers in Dana Meadows, at almost 10,000 feet in elevation, and on Mammoth Peak well after the Tioga Road opens for the season, usually in late May. "Suncups" pock the surface.*

Wilderness offers ▲
*backpackers solitude and
spiritual refreshment—the
"tonic" of wild places.
Where heavy use ruts a
trail, hikers often walk
alongside the route,
ultimately creating parallel
paths. The scars may
require decades to heal,
for the growing
season is short.*

▲ **In Tuolumne Meadows, at 8,600 feet the Sierra's largest subalpine**
*meadow, standing water from recent snowmelt mirrors the unglaciated
summits of Unicorn Peak (center) and the Cockscomb. Wet meadows are
especially fragile and vulnerable to impacts.*

◀ **The deeply** weathered granite on Medlicott Dome above Lower Cathedral Lake suggests glaciation was insufficient to smooth the irregular surface. Fine-grained feldspar crystals armor the humps, confirming the relative resistance of different minerals to wind and water. The summit of Tresidder Peak, named for the long-time president of the Yosemite Park and Curry Co., escaped glacial ice.

Life in the Harsh Sierra

JOHN DITTLI

▲ **I**nhabiting rockslides, the wary, reclusive pika, a relative of rabbits, dries and stores herbaceous plants to sustain itself over the long high-country winter under deep snow.

▼ **T**he succulent, fleshy leaves of stonecrop store water, an adaptation to the intense summer sunlight and desiccating winds of high, rocky slopes. Survival under these harsh conditions, where moisture is precious, demands water conservation.

BOB RONEY

▲ **P**referring streamsides, the adaptable Pacific treefrog, shown nestled in an aster, ranges from the Central Valley of California to near treeline.

JIM AND LYNN WILSON

▲ **T**he brilliant hues of wildflowers, such as the pink monkey flower, speckle park meadows and streambanks.

BOB RONEY

◀ **T**he blood-red saprophytic snow plant emerges from the forest floor soon after the snow melts.

▲ *Cradled in the shadow of aptly named Ragged Peak, its stark summit crag untouched by glacial ice,* *the three Young Lakes, in bowl-like cirques at about 9,900 feet in elevation, embody the bold, yet serene, essence of alpine wilderness. Weathering along vertical joints has flaked the mountain's granite and sharpened its toothy spire. Lupines add contrasting color to the lower lake's shoreline.*

LARRY ULRICH

◄ *"**F**retting the air
into music,"* in the words
of John Muir, the "tuneful
and joyful" Tuolumne
River cascades
down California Falls
in symphonic
extravagance.
Proclaimed a Wild and
Scenic River in 1984, the
Tuolumne drains the
northern half of the park.
Cloud-seeding over the
watershed, started in
1990 by San Joaquin
Valley water interests,
will adversely affect
ecological patterns and
relationships.

ED COOPER

The namesake ▷
dome of early
Tuolumne Meadows
settler and goatherd
John Baptist Lembert is
a classic *roche
moutonnée* (sheep's
back)—smoothly
sloped on the glacial
upstream side and
steeply jagged
downstream.

To Hetch Hetchy—The Other Yosemite Valley

From its ▷ origins along the Sierra crest, the Tuolumne River merges countless tributaries into a vibrant artery that courses through the deeply gorged Grand Canyon of the Tuolumne and leads backpackers to Hetch Hetchy.

FRED HIRSCHMANN

ED COOPER

▲ **K**olana Rock soars above bathtub-ringed
Hetch Hetchy Reservoir. O'Shaughnessy Dam,
authorized by the Raker Act in 1913, completed in
1923, and heightened in the 1930s, impounded the
Tuolumne River—within the already-established
park—and inundated a saddened Muir's "other
Yosemite" to supply water and power
to San Francisco.

◀ **"D**am Hetch Hetchy!" Muir wrote. "As well
dam for water-tanks the people's cathedrals and
churches, for no holier temple has ever been
consecrated by the heart of man." Its similarity to
Yosemite Valley is striking—a glaciated canyon,
waterfalls (Wapama Falls, center), domes, even a
near-facsimile of El Capitan and nesting peregrine
falcons. Its name is derived from a Miwok word for a
native grass. A recent controversial proposal to drain
and restore Hetch Hetchy died,
lacking adequate political support.

▲ **T**he meaning of Tueeulala Falls's
name, like Wapama's, is unknown. Fleeting
and appearing delicate, the spray drops
about 1,000 feet from the cliff's prow until the
stream dries in mid-summer.

GAIL BANDINI

The Big Trees

Virtually every possible superlative has probably been bestowed on the giant sequoia, also called Big Tree and Sierra redwood. Notable for its longevity, some reaching more than 3,000 years of age, and its height—some specimens surpass 30-story buildings—*Sequoiadendron giganteum* is neither the oldest living thing nor the tallest. Rather, it is the behemoth's colossal size that inspires reverence and wonder—even disbelief. In sheer volume it is the world's largest lifeform. Once more widely distributed, naturally seeded giant sequoias are now confined to 75 isolated groves on the Sierra Nevada's western flank. Most of the groves, having escaped nineteenth-century logging, are now protected. Three lie within Yosemite's boundaries. The Mariposa Grove, a legacy of the Yosemite Grant located near the park's south entrance, is the largest and most accessible. The big trees of either the Merced or Tuolumne grove were probably the first seen by non-Indian people, members of the Joseph Walker party who crossed the Sierra in 1833. A mature sequoia may annually produce 2,000 cones that cling, tightly closed, to the branches for years until a feeding chickaree (Douglas squirrel), a tiny boring beetle, or the heat of a fire dries the cones, thus releasing the seeds that resemble oat flakes. In fact, a regime of occasional fires is vital to sequoia reproduction. To survive, sequoias must be vigorous and tenacious. Even in death they persist. The wood, though brittle, resists decay, and relics remain on the ground for centuries.

▲ **The massive butt swell of a sequoia** magnifies the sense of feeling dwarfed. The tree's root system, spreading 100-150 feet around the base only 2 to 5 feet beneath the surface, is vulnerable to excessive trampling, which compacts and erodes soil.

Enshrouded by fog that enhances the grove's ▷ cathedral-like atmosphere, the Grizzly Giant, about 2,700 years old, may be the oldest living big tree. Topped repeatedly by lightning and scarred by countless fires, the mammoth trunk stands "only" 209 feet tall but is almost 31 feet across at its base. The large elbowed branch 95 feet up the trunk is 6 feet in diameter.

GRIZZLY
GIANT

FRED HIRSCHMANN

▲ *Thick, spongy bark and tannin-rich* wood retard burning, enabling sequoias to survive most fires. This furrowed pillar towers over the Mariposa Grove Museum, the site where Galen Clark, first guardian of the Yosemite Grant, built a cabin in the early 1860s. Clark first brought public attention to the grove, here mantled by fresh snow that enhances the trees' stately nobility.

Land of Many Trees

▼ **With roundish leaves that quiver in even a** light breeze, thin-barked quaking aspens dapple the high country with splashes of gold in the fall. The only deciduous tree in the subalpine forest, sun-loving aspens grow in clonal groves, sprouting chiefly from single root systems rather than seeds.

▲ **The lovely spring blossoms of the** moisture-loving Pacific dogwood, its deciduous leaves not fully developed, and the reddish, creased bark of a staunch incense-cedar—not a true cedar—adorn the banks of the brimming Merced River in Yosemite Valley. Both shade-tolerant and abundant, the two species share a common range at low to middle elevations. The dogwood's prominent bracts—not petals— embrace the inconspicuous central flowers that ripen in the fall into succulent crimson fruits favored by birds.

◀ **A robust tree, the western juniper attains exceptional girth in relation to its height. Growing** sparsely on domes and crags, in rock crevices rather than a soil substrate, gnarled junipers tolerate austerities that other conifers cannot survive. Exposed to blistering winds and blizzards, generous snowfall, intense sunlight, and dry summers, they may reach an age of 3,000 years! Birds play a crucial role in dispersing their seeds.

People at Yosemite

Preserve or playground? Wilderness or resort? Recreation or re-creation? Ask a random sampling of the 3.5 million people who now visit the park each year what the Yosemite experience should be, and the answers reflect diverse perceptions and values. To some Yosemite is a hallowed sanctuary; to others a recreational mecca; to many a magical, variable blend of active discovery and passive interaction. By almost anyone's yardstick, though, it is special. Native people first inhabited this setting about 4,000 years ago, living in tune with the land. The arrival of non-Indian people in the mid-nineteenth century forever changed their lifeways—and the destiny of Yosemite itself. Explorers and trappers came first, then miners and settlers. After the Mariposa Battalion's incursion into Yosemite Valley in 1851, word spread about the valley's stupendous scenery.

In 1855 the first tourist parties entered the valley, and settlers and entrepreneurs soon followed. The tales of incredible splendor attracted artists, photographers, writers, and promoters who extolled Yosemite's grandeur. Hotels and homesteads sprouted, and visitation blossomed. So did efforts to preserve its beauty. The landmark Yosemite Grant in 1864, the genesis of the park movement, set aside Yosemite Valley and the Mariposa Grove to be administered by the State of California for "...public use, resort and recreation." On October 1, 1890, Congress designated Yosemite as "reserved forest lands," making it now the nation's third-oldest national park. Over the ensuing century park managers have continually grappled with the dilemma of balancing visitor use with resource preservation.

▼ **Spray churned up by Vernal Fall in spring and early summer drenches both hikers and the** luxuriant vegetation on the popular Mist Trail, a 1.5-mile walk from the valley floor to the top. Even a short stroll away from the trappings of civilization kindles a closer personal connection with the intrinsic rhythms of nature.

A *lavish winter* ▲
*panorama of Yosemite Valley
and the High Sierra
wilderness spreads out a
visual and emotional feast for
a cross-country skier at
Dewey Point, located across
the valley from El Capitan.
Snow buffers noise,
amplifying the sounds of
silence, and protects life
beneath its blanket
of insulation.*

◀ **U**sing the technical gear
*needed for safety and support, rock
climbers painstakingly and
methodically scale the near-vertical
northwest face of Half Dome. Since
the pioneering ascent in 1957, the
2,000-foot wall has challenged skilled
climbers to chart a number of routes.
As climbing has grown in popularity,
impacts on cliffs have increased.
"Clean" climbing techniques
developed in recent years greatly
reduce damage to rocks. The
Yosemite Mountaineering School
offers professional
climbing instruction.*

ED COOPER

"Seeing" the Valley

DIANNE DIETRICH LEIS

▲ ▶ **W**hether through a camera's eye from ground level or with a bird's-eye view from above, people are spiritually—and sometimes physically—uplifted by the valley's expressive dynamics. Inspired by lens-artists such as Ansel Adams, serious photographers diligently pursue their craft, while snapshooters seek mementos of their experiences. Qualified hang-glider pilots are permitted to fly from Glacier Point early on summer mornings.

DICK DIETRICH

◀ **R**iding on a paved bikeway obscured here by meadow grass, bicyclists enjoy exercise and a delightful way to experience the valley. Bicycles afford alternative transportation that relieves traffic congestion in the valley on busy days, but off surfaced routes they denude vegetation and create unsightly scars in meadows and woodlands.

▲ **Seeing, feeling, being—the most personal Yosemite encounter. Standing on the** footbridge below Lower Yosemite Fall, immersed in its baptism, watch the prismatic play of light in its spray. On a spring night, under a full moon, revel in its "moonbow." Listen to its bellowing roar. With "Nature streaming into us" (John Muir), let your sense of wonder soar, and feel your kinship with the Earth.

41

PETER FRENCH

▲ *Two-hour Valley Floor Tours, scheduled several times daily year-round, offer visitors an* interpretive overview of the valley's significant features. Easy and convenient, especially for visitors with tight time constraints or walking impairments, this narrated trip is a service of the park's prime concessioner. Open-air trams are used during warm weather, enclosed buses when temperatures cool.

◀ *The baronial* Ahwahnee Hotel opened in 1927 in Yosemite Valley. Constructed of native stone and wood, the Ahwahnee (the Miwok name for the valley, meaning "place of the gaping mouth") was built at the direction of National Park Service Director Stephen Mather as a luxury accommodation for wealthy guests.

GAIL BANDINI

A Place for All of Us

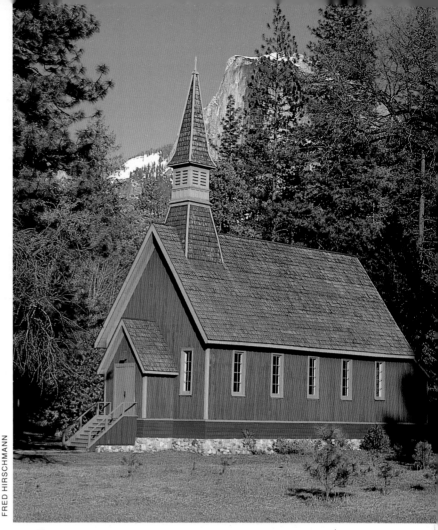

FRED HIRSCHMANN

Legendary naturalist Carl Sharsmith, who has spent almost every summer in Yosemite since 1930, shares his discovery and love of nature's little things with a group of children, tomorrow's voters and park advocates.

Built in 1879 near the base of the Four-Mile Trail, the picturesque Yosemite Chapel is the site of regularly scheduled worship services and numerous weddings. Relocated to the Old Village in 1901, the structure is the park's second-oldest building in continuous use.

DICK DIETRICH

Serendipitous encounters, often simple and sometimes close, are exciting moments. Stay alert and attuned to your surroundings. When nature crosses your path, don't miss it.

◀ **T**he use of horses is traditional in western national parks, predating the parks themselves. Other than the flat-brimmed hat, nothing seems more symbolic of the National Park Service than a ranger on horseback. Well-trained horses tolerant of people can take patrol rangers to places where vehicles can't—at a faster pace than a person on foot.

RAYE SANTOS

▼ **R**anger-led interpretive activities add a dimension of understanding, discovery, and enrichment to a park experience. Professionally conducted walks such as the short Sentinel Dome hike, evening talks, and cultural programs emphasize resource values, park use ethics, and stewardship.

DIANNE DIETRICH LEIS

SUGGESTED READING

ARNO, STEPHEN F., et al. *Discovering Sierra Trees* (also *Birds, Mammals, and Reptiles and Amphibians*). Three Rivers and Yosemite, California: Sequoia Natural History Association and Yosemite Association, 1974-1985.

BROWNING, PETER. *Yosemite Place Names.* Lafayette, California: Great West Books, 1988.

HUBER, N. KING. *The Geologic Story of Yosemite National Park.* Yosemite, California: Yosemite Association, 1989; reprint of U.S. Geological Survey Bulletin 1595, U.S. Government Printing Office, Washington, D.C., 1987.

JONES, WILLIAM R. *Yosemite: The Story Behind the Scenery.* Las Vegas, Nevada: KC Publications, Inc., 1989 (revised edition).

NATIONAL PARK SERVICE. *Yosemite: Official National Park Handbook.* Washington D.C.: U.S. Government Printing Office, 1990.

Note: Any book written by John Muir is recommended.

YOSEMITE NATIONAL PARK

Mount Conness

GRAND CANYON OF THE TUOLUMNE RIVER

To Lee Vining

Tioga Pass Entrance

Mount Dana

Lembert Dome

Mather

White Wolf

Mount Hoffmann

Tioga Road

TUOLUMNE MEADOWS

John Muir Trail

Cathedral Peak

Pacific Crest Trail

S-120

Big Oak Flat Entrance

TUOLUMNE GROVE

MERCED GROVE

• Mount Watkins

Clouds Rest

North Dome

Yosemite Falls

Half Dome

Mount Lyell •

LITTLE YOSEMITE VALLEY

Ribbon Fall

El Capitan

YOSEMITE VALLEY

Glacier Point

Bridalveil Fall

Taft Point

• Mount Starr King

CLARK RANGE

Arch Rock Entrance

El Portal

S-140 To Merced

Chinquapin

Badger Pass

1 Kilometer

1 Mile

▲ NORTH

• Wawona

South Entrance **MARIPOSA GROVE**

S-41 To Fresno

VICINITY MAP

PACIFIC OCEAN

• Carson City

5

395

San Francisco

YOSEMITE NATIONAL PARK

NEVADA

N

CALIFORNIA

5

395

DIANNE DIETRICH LEIS

The model pioneered in 1864 with the Yosemite Grant and reaffirmed in 1872 with the establishment of Yellowstone National Park has been validated around the world. About 120 nations now have reserves called national parks. Yosemite, its centennial just past, is a paragon of that concept, but over the past 100 years the park has been relentlessly stressed. Turmoil and controversy have been constant companions. Yet, despite the political turbulence that continues to this day, this treasure has remained relatively unscathed, exemplifying stability and continuity in a rapidly changing society. It epitomizes not only our cultural value systems and priorities, but also the wisdom inherent in the preservation ethic. As Yosemite enters its second century, that wisdom—indeed, vision—is paramount. Internal and external pressures impinge on its integrity and its future. To address those issues with clarity and resolution requires rededication to the ideals of resource stewardship "...for the enjoyment of future generations."

Tenaya Canyon typifies "The wonder of the world, the beauty and the power..." inscribed on an ancient English gravestone.

CARR CLIFTON

▲ **S**ubjected to unremitting adversities and impoverished growing conditions, this *stunted, wind-blasted Jeffrey pine, possibly several hundred years old, defines tenacity and adaptability.*

Inside back cover: *This* ▷ *stunning portrayal of Yosemite Valley rivals a nineteenth-century Albert Bierstadt painting. Photo by Ed Cooper.*

Back cover: *Regal giant* ▷ *sequoias, like Yellowstone's Old Faithful, symbolize national park values. Photo by Russ Finley.*

NEW: In Pictures — The Continuing Story: Bryce Canyon, Death Valley, Everglades, Glen Canyon-Lake Powell, Grand Canyon, Mount Rainier, Mount St. Helens, Petrified Forest, Sequoia-Kings Canyon, Yellowstone, Yosemite, Zion.
Books in the Story Behind the Scenery book series: Acadia, Alcatraz Island, Arches, Blue Ridge Parkway, Bryce Canyon, Canyon de Chelly, Canyonlands, Cape Cod, Capitol Reef, Channel Islands, Civil War Parks, Colonial, Crater Lake, Death Valley, Denali, Devils Tower, Dinosaur, Everglades, Fort Clatsop, Gettysburg, Glacier, Glen Canyon-Lake Powell, Grand Canyon, Grand Canyon-North Rim, Grand Teton, Great Basin, Great Smoky Mountains, Haleakala, Hawaii Volcanoes, Independence, Lake Mead-Hoover Dam, Lassen Volcanic, Lincoln Parks, Mammoth Cave, Mount Rainier, Mount Rushmore, Mount St. Helens, National Park Service, National Seashores, North Cascades, Olympic, Petrified Forest, Redwood, Rocky Mountain, Scotty's Castle, Sequoia-Kings Canyon, Shenandoah, Statue of Liberty, Theodore Roosevelt, Virgin Islands, Yellowstone, Yosemite, Zion.

Published by KC Publications · Box 14883 · Las Vegas, NV 89114

Printed by Dong-A Printing and Publishing, Seoul, Korea
Color Separations by Kedia/Kwangyangsa Co., Ltd.